Dawn S

The Old Warrior

Illustrated by Ann Baum

Series editor: Rod Nesbitt

This book is dedicated to my husband, Giovanni and my children, Gina, Michele and Gian-Marco for their encouragement. Also to the memory of Ian Bompas and Elizabeth Crompton-Lomax who helped a dream become a reality.

Heinemann Educational
A division of Heinemann Publishers (Oxford) Ltd
Halley Court, Jordan Hill, Oxford OX2 8EJ

Heinemann Educational Boleswa
PO Box 10103, Village Post Office, Gaborone, Botswana
Heinemann Educational Books (Nigeria) Ltd
PMB 5205, Ibadan

LONDON EDINBURGH PARIS MADRID
ATHENS BOLOGNA MELBOURNE
SYDNEY AUCKLAND PORTSMOUTH (NH)
SINGAPORE TOKYO

© Dawn Smargiassi 1993
First published by Heinemann Educational in 1993

British Library Cataloguing in Publication Data
A catalogue record for this book is available from the British Library

ISBN 0 435 892363

The right of Dawn Smargiassi to be identified as the author of this work has been asserted by her in accordance with the Copyright, Designs and Patents Act 1988

Glossary
Difficult words are listed alphabetically on page 60

Printed and bound in Great Britain by
Cox & Wyman Ltd, Reading, Berkshire

93 94 95 10 9 8 7 6 5 4 3 2 1

Chapter One

Farmer van der Riet's land lay beneath the Drakensberg Mountains. It stretched acre after acre far to the north and east. Through the farm flowed a broad gentle river. The farmer's house stood close to the river in the valley. The colourful huts of the Zulu workers were spread out across the hills high above the farmhouse.

This was where Mfeni lived with his family. Their hut was larger than any of the others, because Mfeni's father was the *Induna* of the farm. The young Zulu boy was very proud of his tall, strong father. They had a happy family. There was his mother, Thandi, who was very beautiful, and his baby sister, Madumbe, who was a nuisance at times. Finally there was his grey-haired grandfather, Sipho.

The family were sitting outside their hut eating their evening meal. The sun was just setting, lighting the great mountains with rays of red and gold.

Tonight Mfeni wanted to discuss something serious with his father. He sat for a long time before he was able to start.

'*Baba*...?'

His father looked at him and nodded.

The family were sitting outside their hut eating their evening meal.

'*Baba*, it's about Madumbe,' Mfeni said.

Zonke looked across at Thandi. They carefully hid their smiles, for they knew what Mfeni wanted to talk about.

'What about Madumbe, my son?' his father asked.

Mfeni did not want to make his father angry. He tried to find the right words.

'Well, speak up, *umfana*,' said his grandfather.

'Give him time, *Baba*,' Mfeni's father said. 'Take your time, my son.'

'Well, *Baba*,' Mfeni began, 'I wondered if I could go out again with the cattle tomorrow morning?'

He quickly ate some more food. He was very unhappy. He knew that Zulu children never argued with their parents.

His grandfather laughed quietly through his white beard.

'So my grandson no longer wants to look after his baby sister?' he said.

Mfeni looked down at his food and waited. When his father spoke, Mfeni stared at him in amazement.

'Well, my son, I will ask your mother if one of the girls can stay home from work in the fields tomorrow.'

'Oh, thank you, *Baba*, thank you…'

'Wait,' said his father, 'I only said I would ask your mother if she could help. But tell me, why do you no longer want to help your sister?'

Before Mfeni could answer, his grandfather began to laugh.

'I have heard the other herd-boys teasing my grandson,' he said. 'Haven't I, *umfana*?'

'Yes, *Ukhulu*,' said Mfeni unhappily.

Zonke put his arm round his son's shoulders.

'Don't let them annoy you, my son,' Zonke said. 'They have all helped to look after younger brothers and sisters.'

'Thulani is the worst,' Mfeni said quietly. 'I think he hates me.'

'Now, my son,' his father replied, 'you must understand that Thulani is very unhappy. He has no mother and he does not see his father very often. Remember his mother died when he was a baby, and his father works in the fields all day. When his father visits his friends, Thulani is all alone. He has no grandfather or sister to talk to him.'

Mfeni nodded, but he could not forget Thulani's bad behaviour. Thulani was the only *umfana* on the farm who made him really angry.

His mother started to tidy up the area around the fire. Grandfather Sipho was sitting in his favourite place beneath the orange tree. He rested his old bones on a flat river rock. Mfeni went and sat next to him. He watched as the old man filled his pipe with tobacco.

'So, my grandson,' his grandfather smiled, 'how long are you going to allow Thulani to upset you?'

'What can I do, *Ukhulu*?' Mfeni asked sadly.

'Tell him he must stop,' his grandfather said. 'If he doesn't, you must fight him.'

'But, *Ukhulu*,' Mfeni replied, 'he is twice as tall as I am.'

'Ah, this is a coward I hear,' his grandfather said. 'At your age we youths had already killed our first leopard.'

Mfeni looked away from his grandfather's angry face. His *Ukhulu* must have been very brave when he was young, he thought. Grandfather Sipho sighed and scratched his head. He touched his *Isicoco*, his head-ring. Made of wood from the gum tree, it showed that he was old and wise. The ring gleamed black in the shadows.

'Now listen to me, Mfeni,' his grandfather said, 'if Thulani starts again tomorrow, you must stand up to him. I don't want people to say my grandson is a coward. Don't start the argument, but don't allow him to tease you.'

'My father will be very angry if he hears we have

been fighting,' said Mfeni. 'And the *Inkosi* van der Riet doesn't like us fighting in the fields.'

The old man spat into the long grass beside the tree.

'Bah!' he said. 'Your father has become too civilised. He no longer enjoys life, but sits around all day like an old woman. Besides,' he went on, pointing his pipe at the farmhouse in the valley, 'I can remember the father of the *Inkosi* van der Riet. Now there was a good friend. His son is just like your father. They've both become old women.'

The old man and the boy sat silently as twilight stole over the valley. The great mountains darkened until they were silhouetted against the sky, like a long line of giant castles.

'Tomorrow,' thought Mfeni, 'if that big bully teases me, I will fight him. I'll fight him like grandfather fought his leopards when he was young.' Suddenly he felt very brave.

Old Sipho smiled as he remembered long ago. He and old Farmer van der Riet would camp for weeks in the mountains and hunt together. Those were good days. But it was also good to sit beneath the orange tree with his grandson beside him and smoke his pipe.

Chapter Two

Next morning Mfeni was playing with his baby sister when his father came into the hut.

'Your mother is sending an *intombi* to look after your sister,' he said, 'so hurry up and get the goats and cattle out.'

Mfeni gave a shout of joy and ran quickly out of the hut. Madumbe shouted angrily for Mfeni to come back and then started to cry. Zonke picked her up and carried her outside.

'He's forgotten his midday meal,' Sipho called, holding up a billy-can.

Zonke whistled loudly down the valley. The small figure stopped on the narrow winding path. He ran quickly back when he saw his father wave. In a few minutes a dozen herd-boys drove bleating goats and mooing cattle out of their pens and into the open field. Sharp whistles and the smack of sticks on the animals' rumps echoed along the valley as the herds were driven up the hill to the grazing grounds.

Mfeni ran from one end of the herd to the other trying to keep the goats together. His father was rich and owned twice as many goats and cattle as the other men. Mfeni was soon joined by the other young boys all driving their herds in the same direction. They shouted greetings to each other.

Thulani was there too, of course. He laughed loudly when he saw Mfeni, pointing his long stick in his direction.

'*Sawubona*, little boy,' he called. 'Why are you not looking after your baby sister today?'

'Today, Thulani, I'm a herder,' he replied. 'From now on Mafuta's daughter will nurse my sister.'

'You're too young to be a herd-boy, Mfeni,' laughed Thulani. 'Herding is for older boys like us.' He pointed to two of his friends.

'I'm not too young,' said Mfeni angrily.

'Just look at you,' sneered Thulani. 'You're all bones and you're no taller than my knee. You're only a child.'

The other herd-boys watched eagerly. They all liked to see a good fight. Skinny Mfeni was standing up to Thulani. He did not seem to be afraid of the big herd-boy.

'Wait until we reach the grazing grounds,' he said angrily. 'I'll show you what no-flesh-on-the-bones can do.'

'Be careful, little one,' the other boy laughed. 'Don't threaten a man.'

The herds climbed over the top of the hill and soon reached the grazing grounds. The cattle quietly started to eat the long grass. The goats, who had run and chased each other all the way, lay in the sun. The young boys threw themselves down under some willow trees at the side of a clear stream. Some of them put their billy-cans in the cool water and then turned to watch Thulani and Mfeni. The older boy looked down at the younger who was a head shorter than he was.

'Now repeat what you said at the kraals,' he ordered, leaning on his stick.

The other boys were very quiet.

'I'm tired of you, Thulani,' Mfeni said bravely. 'You'll never leave me alone.'

'Poor little boy,' Thulani said, prodding Mfeni with his stick. 'You're only a child. Why don't you go home?'

Thulani strutted around Mfeni like a peacock. He looked at his friends and laughed loudly.

'I'm not a child,' screamed Mfeni in a rage, 'and I'm going to show you.'

He picked up his two fighting sticks. Thulani did the same. Mfeni beat his sticks together and chanted war-cries Sipho had taught him. He started to move toward Thulani. Then, with a frightening shout, he raised one stick high and charged at Thulani.

The older boy raised his stick just in time and the sticks crashed together. The boys jumped back,

Mfeni raised one stick high and charged at Thulani.

holding their sticks tightly in their hands. Mfeni rocked from side to side, his legs apart and his feet firmly on the ground. He watched Thulani carefully, ready to strike if he saw a chance.

Thulani was really afraid now. He held his sticks up in front of him in an X shape to protect his head and shoulders.

The rest of the herd-boys had formed a circle around the two stick fighters. They were shouting instructions at the one they wanted to win.

Thulani lowered his arms for a moment and Mfeni brought his right-hand stick crashing down. It broke Thulani's stick in two and caught the older boy across the nose. Blood came from Thulani's nose as he fell back. He got quickly to his feet and found his other stick.

The herd-boys jumped and shouted in excitement. The noise frightened the goats and they ran off in all directions bleating loudly.

Thulani ran at Mfeni, his stick ready. They hit each other on the body, the noise of the sticks sounding like the cracks of whips. Although Thulani got a few blows in, Mfeni was very quick and many more missed. He hit Thulani hard many times and Thulani soon started to get tired. His body was aching, his nose was bleeding and he was becoming more and more afraid.

Mfeni brought his stick crashing down again and caught Thulani across the legs. Thulani fell with a cry of pain. He tried to get up, but Mfeni dropped his sticks and dived at the older boy. They rolled over and over, punching at each other wildly.

Now Mfeni's nose was bleeding and he had a sore eye. Apart from his bleeding nose, both of Thulani's eyes were swollen and he had a broken tooth. Thulani was exhausted, but Mfeni did not stop. He punched Thulani again and again. Finally the other boys pulled him away and held him down until he became calm. Thulani lay on his back and cried with the pain.

Someone poured cold water on Thulani's face. He drank gratefully. He did not care if they were laughing at him, just as long as they kept that skinny little devil away from him.

Chapter Three

Thandi sat on her knees outside the hut making snuff from long tobacco leaves. *Ukhulu* Sipho sat in his usual place, in the shade of the orange tree. He was proudly watching his grandson who was sitting in the doorway of the hut. When his mother looked at him, Mfeni quickly looked the other way.

'Your face is badly swollen, my son,' she said. 'You should sit inside the hut where it is cool.'

'I'm all right, Mama,' he said, then he asked, 'Is *Baba* still angry with me?'

He could not forget how shocked and angry his father had been the afternoon before. When Thulani and he had been helped home, their fathers had to go and bring home the cattle and goats. Then his father and *Ukhulu* Sipho had to milk the cows, all twenty of them.

'You know your father,' she said. 'He doesn't like you to fight and then not be able to do your duties.'

'But, Mama, you know Thulani has been teasing me, and he's always calling me a nursemaid.'

'Well,' she said with a smile, 'I'm sure Thulani will now be wise enough not to call you a nursemaid again.'

'So you're not angry with me for fighting, Mama?' Mfeni asked.

'No, Mfeni,' she replied. 'You had a very good reason to fight Thulani.'

Mfeni stood in front of his mother, his small face very serious.

'Mama,' he said, 'I'll never be ashamed of looking after Madumbe again. And I think you're the best mother and the prettiest of all the women.'

His mother laughed and gently touched his face.

'You'll make your mother very vain,' she said. 'Now go and lie down in the hut.'

'Come and sit with me, brave warrior,' his grandfather called.

'So,' said the old man when Mfeni sat down very carefully beside him, 'how does it feel to be a hero?'

'My father is angry with me, *Ukhulu*, and my face is very sore.'

'Don't worry, little man,' his grandfather said. 'Today your father is a very proud man, and so is your *Ukhulu*. It was like old times seeing a young warrior being helped home from battle. It's a pity the enemy was only a cheeky *umfana* and not a great spotted leopard.'

The old man struck a match and held it to the bowl of his pipe. He puffed at it happily. Mfeni touched his cut lip gently. It was too painful to smile.

'Don't worry,' said *Ukhulu* Sipho, 'those are your battle scars. Be proud of them, for they may be the only ones you'll ever have.'

Mfeni dropped his hand. He would never let his grandfather see how painful his wounds were.

The family had their evening meal outside, around the fire. Madumbe sat close to her brother sharing mouthfuls of meat and *phuthu*. Their dog lay nearby, waiting for scraps of food. Suddenly the dog started to bark and they looked up to see Thulani entering the kraal. When he got closer they could see that his face was badly bruised. Besides cut lips and purple eyes, his nose was very swollen.

'*Sawubona, Ukhulu,*' he greeted the old man first, and then the other members of the family in turn.

'Sit down, Thulani, and share our meal,' said Thandi.

'I thank you, *Anti*,' he replied very politely, 'but I have just shared a meal with my father.'

He looked at Mfeni who was sitting staring at him. Thulani smiled and then looked away. He looked back again and Mfeni tried to smile at him, but it was very painful.

It was too painful to smile.

'Mfeni,' Thulani said, 'your father named you well, for not only do you look like a monkey, but you move as fast as one too.'

Mfeni had never heard Thulani speak like this before.

'Thulani,' he replied, 'your name means keep quiet, but you never know when to do so.' He did not notice the sudden smile on his grandfather's face.

'I have come here tonight, Mfeni,' said Thulani, 'to tell you that you are much better than a herd-boy. You are already a young man. I want to apologise for the way I have behaved.'

Mfeni did not know where to look. He coughed, got up, and then sat down again. His mother quickly tried to help him. She got up and looked closely at Thulani's face.

'No one has put medicine on your cuts,' she said.

'My father hasn't had the time,' Thulani replied.

'Come,' Thandi said, 'I will bathe them in the hut where I keep my herbs and medicines.'

Grandfather Sipho watched as Thulani was led away by his daughter-in-law.

'So the enemy has come over to my little man,' he said.

'*Baba*, you are only making matters worse,'

Zonke said quickly.

'You've become an old woman, Zonke,' Sipho replied. 'Mfeni and I understand each other.'

Mfeni tried not to smile. His grandfather still lived in a world where the young hunted leopards – no one had seen a leopard on the farm for years. In grandfather's world men still proudly wore loincloths, now only worn by the young. It had taken years to persuade his grandfather to wear trousers instead of his loincloth. Unfortunately, every pair he got, he cut off just below the knees and tied them with strips of leather. The upper part of his body he refused to cover with anything but his dark *isiphuku*. He still thought of himself as a fierce, young Zulu warrior who was afraid of neither man nor animal.

The humble behaviour of Thulani annoyed him. He threw his bone to the dog and wiped his mouth with the back of his hand. He rocked to and fro as he sat and stared into the flames of the open fire.

Chapter Four

It was very early when Mfeni set out along the footpath that ran from the kraals to the farmhouse below. He was wearing a new pair of khaki shorts and a bright scarlet shirt. His feet were bare, for he still could not wear shoes. They were too heavy and they stopped him from running freely.

From farther up the hill his old enemy and now his friend, Thulani, watched enviously. He wished he could go to fetch the *Inkosi*'s children, Dirkie and Helena, from boarding school. He had always wanted to ride in the open Land Rover as Mfeni did. But he knew that Mfeni had grown up with Dirkie as Grandfather Sipho and the old farmer had grown up together.

When Dirkie was home, Mfeni saw him every day after they had finished their duties. Then they would go fishing or hunting.

The blue Land Rover appeared from behind the house, its horn hooting. Mfeni began to run, lifting his stick over his head to wave at Thulani.

He reached the Land Rover, smiling from ear to ear when he greeted the driver.

'*Sawubona, Inkosi.*'

'*Sawubona*, you little monkey-face,' greeted Farmer van der Riet, good-naturedly. 'In you get.'

Mfeni climbed into the passenger seat. Now he could watch the farmer as he moved the gear lever and the steering wheel. One day when he was older, he told himself, he would own one of these Land Rovers and take his *Ukhulu* on long journeys across the country.

'Hey, wake up, little one, and please open the gate.' The farmer's voice made Mfeni jump with surprise.

'*Awu, Inkosi,*' Mfeni said. 'I didn't realise we were already there.'

He held the gate open and the farmer drove through.

'Close it carefully, little one,' Farmer van der Riet called. 'It's bad enough to have our cattle stolen by rustlers, we don't want them to wander off through open gates.'

'My father,' said Mfeni nervously, 'told us that more cattle have been stolen from the farm, *Inkosi.*'

'That is so, Mfeni,' said the farmer. 'But we'll catch them, if we can find their path across the mountains. The one they take the cattle over. Until now they've been too clever for us.'

Farmer van der Riet drove silently for some time. He was thinking about the cattle rustlers. They came over the Drakensberg Mountains after

One day he would own one of these Land Rovers.

nightfall to steal the best cattle and dairy cows. By morning there was no trace of them. They seemed to disappear into the air. The police could find no clues. They kept watch on all the mountain passes, but so far they had seen nothing.

'Tonight,' said the farmer, 'I will speak to your father about this. We must find a way to trap these rustlers.'

'*Yebo, Inkosi*,' Mfeni said.

Suddenly the big farmer began to laugh.

'Don't you worry about the rustlers. Leave that to your father and me,' he said. 'Just enjoy the ride. It won't be long before we have Dirkie and Helena with us.'

Mfeni smiled back happily. It would be good to have Dirkie back home again.

Chapter Five

Grandfather Sipho sat beneath his *isiphuku*, his calabash of beer between his feet. He lifted the calabash and took a drink from the narrow neck. He licked his lips and sat back against the orange tree. Then he heard voices coming up the path from the valley.

In a few minutes Farmer van der Riet appeared, followed by Mfeni and the two van der Riet children. Dirkie was tall and fair-haired like his father. Helena looked like her mother. She was small, dark-haired and very pretty.

Their father greeted Sipho as one greets a warrior of his age. The old man sat, looking up at the tall farmer, remembering days long ago.

'Mama,' said Mfeni, 'Helena has come to see Madumbe.'

As Thandi led Helena into the hut, Zonke came out and joined the little group beside Sipho. The men had serious business to discuss.

'Tell me, Zonke,' asked the farmer, 'why wasn't Intambo on the farm today?'

Zonke looked surprised. He was the *Induna* and he was in charge of all the workers on the farm.

'*Habe, Inkosi,*' he replied, 'he was here all day. He was in charge of gathering the hay.'

Farmer van der Riet shook his head.

'No, Zonke,' he said, 'he was at the village this afternoon. I saw him myself. Mfeni and Dirkie saw him too. There were a number of Basuto there with mules. They were buying supplies. Intambo was talking to them.'

'There must be a mistake,' Zonke said.

'No, there's no mistake,' replied van der Riet. 'And when I went to speak to him, he just disappeared.'

'I've told you about Intambo many times,' *Ukhulu* Sipho said to Zonke, 'but you would never listen to me. I never did trust that young fox.'

'But what was he doing talking to the Basuto?' asked Zonke. 'We have nothing to do with them.'

Farmer van der Riet scratched his head.

'I think I have an idea,' he said, 'but we won't talk about that now. I'll talk to Intambo in the morning.'

'Too many cattle have disappeared from the farm,' said Sipho to the farmer. 'If your father had been alive, we would have caught them by now.'

'*Awu, Baba*,' said Zonke angrily, 'we have searched every road and found nothing. Even the police have found nothing.'

Farmer van der Riet smiled at the grey-haired

old man who had spent most of his life with his own father. The *Inkosi* took a pouch of tobacco and handed it to Sipho. It was something he had done for many years.

'Well, I must take the children home. They'll be tired,' the farmer said. He called the children and then took his leave of the once great warrior, Sipho Dlamini.

'We'll go riding tomorrow, Dirkie,' Mfeni shouted.

'Right,' Dirkie called back.

On the way home Farmer van der Riet took his children past the paddock. Dirkie wanted to see his horse. It came quickly when the boy whistled. It licked his face and skipped with happiness, its hooves pawing at the ground.

'We'll go out tomorrow,' Dirkie said, 'with Mfeni.'

The horse raced off into the darkness and the family walked back to the farmhouse.

The next morning was the van der Riet children's first morning at home.

'What are you going to do today, children?' their mother asked as she gave them plates of porridge.

'First I'm going to go for a ride,' answered Dirkie, 'with Mfeni.'

Before anyone could speak again, the door opened and Farmer van der Riet came in. Zonke was right behind him.

'What's the matter?' his wife said, when she saw how worried he looked.

He looked at Dirkie and wiped his hand across his forehead.

'Children,' he said very quietly, 'please go to your bedrooms. I'll speak to you both later.'

The children quietly left the kitchen. Zonke went out and closed the kitchen door. He sat on the steps at the back verandah. The saddles for the horses hung over the verandah rail.

Van der Riet sat at the table. His wife realised that something serious had happened. Finally he looked up.

'It's Dirkie's horse,' he said.

'Has it been stolen?' his wife asked.

'If only that was all!' the farmer replied.

'Pieter, what has happened?' Mrs van der Riet asked.

'The rustlers were here again last night!'

'Oh no, Pieter,' Jane van der Riet cried.

'Yes, they stole ten of my best Jersey cows,' her husband said. 'But they also frightened Dirkie's horse. It tried to jump the fence, but it fell and broke its leg.'

'Oh Pieter,' his wife cried.

'You know what I have to do, don't you?' he asked.

'Can't you try to save it?'

'There's nothing we can do,' he replied.

A sudden noise made them look up. Dirkie was standing in the doorway. He stared at his father with tears in his eyes.

'Oh no, Pa, please,' he cried. When he saw the look on his father's face, he turned and ran down the passage.

'What about the men you left on guard?' asked Jane van der Riet. 'Are they all right?'

'The rustlers knocked them out and tied them up,' her husband replied. 'But they're all right now.'

Outside Zonke sat with his head in his hands. The noise of someone lifting a saddle made him look up.

'What are you doing here, *Baba*?' Mfeni asked in surprise.

Zonke stood up and took the saddle from his son.

'You won't be riding today, my son,' he said, as he put the saddle back on the rail.

'What's happened, *Baba*?' Mfeni asked.

Inside the house they could hear the sound of a

The three boys were standing looking sadly down at the horse.

boy crying. Zonke closed his eyes and sighed.

'Come with me, my son,' he said, 'and I will tell you.'

Dirkie bravely went with his father to the place where his horse was lying. Farmer van der Riet had called a veterinary surgeon to examine the horse. He told the father and son he could do nothing.

Mfeni and his father were standing looking sadly down at the horse. Thulani, the son of Intambo, had come too. The three boys stood with tears in their eyes as Farmer van der Riet aimed his rifle. In the farmhouse Jane van der Riet and Helena heard the two rifle shots and knew it was all over.

Chapter Six

Zonke and Thandi helped Thulani to move his clothes and other possessions into their family hut. His father, Intambo, had disappeared and could not be found. The family were very kind to the boy, and they did not mention his father's strange behaviour. But Thulani was very worried. He knew they thought his father was one of the rustlers.

The kindness of Mfeni and his family did not help. He did not know what would happen to him. The farmers would try harder to catch the rustlers now, for cattle-rustling was a terrible crime. Then there was Dirkie van der Riet. Everywhere he went, everyone was talking about the shooting of Dirkie's horse.

Thandi gave Thulani a corner of the hut to sleep in, close to Mfeni and Madumbe. He lay on his *umkhukha*. He had no blanket, for the night was quite warm. The open fire in the centre of the hut threw long shadows on the walls. Outside he could hear Mfeni's family talking quietly to each other.

'Did you see Dirkie tonight, Mfeni?' Thandi asked.

'No, Mama,' he replied. 'The last time I saw him was just after the shooting. The *Inkosi* told me he has locked himself in his room. He won't eat or speak to anyone.'

'That is easily understood,' said *Ukhulu* Sipho. 'A man and his horse can become as close as a father to his son.'

Zonke threw a log on to the fire. He sighed as he took a pinch of snuff from his father.

'Don't be so sad, my husband,' said Thandi gently.

'I made a mistake when I trusted Intambo,' Zonke said. 'My father warned me many times, but I did nothing. What will the *Inkosi* think of me? How can he ever trust me again?'

Thandi started to say something, but *Ukhulu* Sipho spoke first.

'My daughter, bring a calabash of beer,' he said. 'Tonight I must talk to my son.'

Thandi got up and went into the hut. Thulani pretended to be asleep.

'Before my daughter-in-law returns,' Sipho said, 'I want to know what the *Inkosi* is going to do about Thulani.'

'Well, my father, the *Inkosi* has decided that Thulani can stay on the farm if he wants to. But the boy may be happier away from here, where he wouldn't have the shame of his father on his young shoulders. If Intambo is guilty, he will serve a long prison sentence. The *Inkosi* wants Thulani to go to school a few miles away. He will pay the fees.'

Thandi appeared and placed the calabash of cold beer at the old man's side. Then she went back into the hut.

◇

Dirkie walked about for days, not eating much and talking to no one. His family tried to make him smile again, but it was Mfeni who finally succeeded.

He and Dirkie often went hunting for quail in the corn-fields. When they walked through the corn, the birds would fly out cheeping in fright. The boys carried short throwing sticks. If they were very quick, they would sometimes hit the quails with the sticks. That morning Mfeni went out alone and hit a quail. He ran quickly to the farmhouse. He arrived out of breath, his eyes big with excitement.

'*Sawubona*, Mfeni,' Jane van der Riet said. 'What have you got there?'

He grinned and opened the parcel carefully. When Jane saw the little brown bird trying to beat its wings, she gave a little scream.

'It's for Dirkie,' the boy explained.

'I'll call him for you,' Jane said, smiling.

When Dirkie saw the bird, he smiled for the first time in many days.

'Where did you get it?' he asked excitedly.

'In the corn-field,' Mfeni replied. 'They're cutting the corn by the river. There are lots of *intendele* there. Come on, let's go down there.'

'Wait,' said the other boy, 'let me get my *isagila* first.'

In a few moments the two boys were running towards the river, Dirkie's horse forgotten for the morning.

◇

During the second week of the school holidays, Dirkie went to visit Mfeni. He found *Ukhulu* Sipho and the two boys sitting beneath the old man's favourite tree. They were happy to see him, especially *Ukhulu* Sipho.

'*Sawubona*, my son,' Ukhulu greeted him.

'*Sawubona, Ukhulu*,' replied Dirkie respectfully.

'It has been a long time,' said the old man, as Dirkie sat down with his friends.

'Dirkie, can we go camping on the 'Berg this weekend?' Mfeni asked.

Dirkie thought this was a good idea, but Thulani

looked very unhappy. Mfeni saw his friend's face.

'I want you to come too,' he said.

Thulani shouted with pleasure.

'Mfeni, can I really?'

'Yes, of course,' Mfeni replied. 'We will come down to the farmhouse at dawn. It will take time to catch the horses and pack for the weekend.'

Dirkie became very quiet. The old man saw how the talk about the horses had made the boy sad. He quickly began to talk about hunting in the mountains and soon Dirkie was laughing happily again.

Thandi came over with a clay plate of freshly roasted mealie cobs. She offered the plate to their guest first. Dirkie took one and took a big bite.

'This is what I miss at boarding school,' he said. 'Hawu, *Ukhulu*, you don't know how much I hate that place.'

Old Sipho nodded.

'I don't know why children are sent to such places,' he said, sucking loudly on his mealie cob. 'There is nothing better than watching the sun hide its face in the evening, or to sit with a full belly after a hard day's work.'

Dirkie agreed with the old man. But he wanted to be a farmer, and to be a good farmer he would have to learn everything about agriculture.

Chapter Seven

Saturday morning finally arrived. Thulani was so excited he could not stand still. Dirkie was riding his father's horse and the other two boys had brought horses down from the kraal. They had food in their saddle-bags and a billy-can each for water or tea. They were climbing on the horses as the van der Riet family came out to say goodbye.

'All of you, be careful of snakes,' said Jane van der Riet.

'Don't worry,' said her husband, 'they'll be quite safe. There is medicine in Dirkie's saddle-bag. Don't go too far up into the mountains. Remember the rustlers. If you see anything, one of you must ride back here at once.'

Helena gave the boys sticks of biltong.

'OK, Pa, we're off,' said his son. They turned the horses and trotted off up the valley.

'We'll see you tomorrow afternoon,' shouted Farmer van der Riet. 'Remember, don't go too far into the mountains.'

Three hours later, the boys were high up in the foothills of the great mountains. The scenery was very beautiful. The green grasslands were like a huge green carpet, and the wild flowers made splashes of red and yellow and blue. Suddenly

They trotted off up the valley.

there was a rumbling sound in the distance.

'*Mayebabo*,' shouted Mfeni, 'that sounds like a hailstorm.'

'What can we do?' asked Thulani. 'That storm will be here soon.'

'Don't worry, Thulani,' said Dirkie. 'We have nearly reached our cave. We'll be safe there. It's just over that little hill.'

They kicked their horses into a canter, for the first clouds were moving quickly over the mountains. The boys knew they had to get out of the storm. The hailstones could be as big as a man's fist, and they could kill both them and the horses.

Over the top of the hill, they found themselves in a deep valley. On the far side of the valley was a beautiful waterfall. It poured over the edge of the mountain with a loud roaring sound.

'There's the cave,' Mfeni said, pointing at the waterfall.

Mfeni smiled at Dirkie as they saw the look of amazement on Thulani's face. They knew this place well, because they often camped here. Thulani looked at the dark opening in the mountain right beside the waterfall.

'How do we get inside?' he asked. 'There's no way up the mountain.'

'We have to go behind the waterfall,' laughed

Dirkie. Thulani's mouth fell open.

'Behind the waterfall!' he cried. 'But how are we going to do that?'

Mfeni and Dirkie laughed.

'Come on,' Mfeni said, 'we'll show you. We must hurry. The storm is coming.'

Thulani followed the other boys along a pathway that wound its way up the side of the valley. Soon the path was just wide enough for one horse at a time. They climbed closer and closer to the waterfall. Thulani closed his eyes in terror. The sound of the storm was now louder than the noise of the waterfall.

His horse followed the others, but Thulani kept his eyes shut. Water poured down on him and he thought the storm had started. Suddenly his horse stopped.

'Open your eyes, Thulani,' Dirkie told him.

They were behind the waterfall on a wide path. On his left was the wall of the mountain. On his right was the waterfall itself. He could look through the water and still see the valley below. His fear quickly disappeared.

'Where's the cave, Mfeni?' Thulani asked.

Mfeni pointed up the path, which widened as it rose. The horses were tired, because they had travelled for three hours with only one rest. The boys climbed down and walked the horses up the path and into the cave. It was enormous, but it became narrower as it went into the mountain. The floor was dry and there was a pile of firewood against one wall.

'We collected that the last time I was home from school,' Dirkie said.

Suddenly, without any warning, the hailstones came crashing down. They were as big as hens' eggs. The noise frightened the horses and the boys talked to them and patted them.

'*Awu*, we were just in time,' Mfeni said, but no one could hear him.

When the storm passed the boys unsaddled the horses and gave them a good rub down. Thulani looked outside. The only noise was the low thunder of the waterfall. The valley was covered in hailstones which looked like millions of jewels in the golden sunlight.

Thulani and Mfeni walked deeper into the cave, until it became too dark to see clearly.

Suddenly Mfeni put his fingers to his lips.

'Ssshhh,' he said. He was listening carefully now.

'There it is again,' he said.

'What?' asked Thulani, looking frightened.

'Dirkie!' Mfeni called. 'Come here and listen.'

The boys walked the horses up the path and into the cave.

Dirkie ran over and the three of them stood listening.

'What do you hear?' Dirkie asked in a whisper.

'It sounds like cattle,' Mfeni replied.

'It is cattle, Mfeni,' said Dirkie, 'but where are they?'

'I don't like this,' said Thulani. 'Let's leave now.'

'Don't be a baby,' Mfeni said. 'You stay here. Dirkie and I will go deeper into the cave and find out where the sound is coming from.'

'What is at the back of the cave?' asked Thulani.

'I don't know,' replied Mfeni. 'We've never gone right to the back.' Mfeni was feeling frightened now too. Maybe it was the *Izitonga* in the mountain with their ghostly cattle.

'Come on, let's go,' said Dirkie, when they heard more mooing.

'Are you staying here, Thulani?' Mfeni asked.

'Yes, I'll stay and look after the horses,' he replied. 'But please don't be long.'

The two boys walked slowly deeper into the cave. Soon the cave narrowed even more and then it turned a corner. It was very dark now and the sound of the cattle was much closer.

'I don't like this, Mfeni,' Dirkie whispered. He shivered with fear, but he wanted to see where the noise was coming from. They turned another corner and the cave became lighter.

'We must be near the end of the cave,' Dirkie said. 'It's getting brighter and brighter. Let's go back.'

The noise of cattle and sheep and goats was very clear now.

'No,' said Mfeni, 'we're here now. We must find the cattle. They may be the ones the rustlers stole from your Pa and the other farmers.'

They went round two more corners. Suddenly they were standing in a larger cave. Facing them, in the centre of the cave, were more than a dozen men. They were sitting round an open fire cooking their midday meal. They were not from any Zulu tribe, for they had colourful blankets round their shoulders and some of them had the cone-shaped hats worn by the Basuto tribe. The boys could only stand and stare at the men.

◇

Thulani was shaking with fear. Mfeni and Dirkie had been gone for hours and they still had not come back. He was too frightened to go and look for them, and this made him feel ashamed. Then he heard the sound of men's voices, and he knew something had happened to his friends.

The boys could only stand and stare at the men.

He remembered what Farmer van der Riet had told them that morning. He quickly put the bridle back on his horse and rode bareback out of the cave. Five minutes later two Basuto men appeared from the back of the cave. They had come for the horses.

It was growing dark as Thulani rode down the valley away from the cave. His horse had had a good rest and it started to gallop at once. By now, he was certain that his friends had been captured by evil spirits.

Thulani soon came to some trees. He looked all around. He realised that he was lost. He had never been here before and he did not know the way back to the farm. As it became dark, the mountains seemed to get closer and closer.

◇

'Run, Dirkie!' Mfeni shouted in a frightened voice. 'Run!'

But it was too late. Two of the men ran from the fire and held their arms. The men were shouting in Sesuto, but neither Mfeni nor Dirkie understood them.

'Let me go!' Mfeni shouted, kicking at the shins of the man who was holding him. The Basuto shook Mfeni hard and then hit him across the back of the head. Dirkie stood still. He was too frightened to do anything. He knew Mfeni was right. They had found the cattle rustlers.

A tall, thin man came to talk to the boys.

'Intambo!' shouted Mfeni. 'What are you doing here?'

'Don't speak to me like that,' Intambo said in a fierce voice.

'Because of what you did,' Mfeni said bravely, 'Dirkie's horse had to be shot.'

For a moment Intambo looked sad. Then he gave a laugh.

'I'm not interested in a horse,' he said. 'We have important things to do.'

'Wait until my father catches you,' Mfeni shouted angrily. 'You won't escape.'

'Please, Mfeni,' said Dirkie, 'please be quiet. These men will only hurt us.'

'You're right,' laughed Intambo, 'you can disappear in the mountains and no one will ever find you.'

Two of the rustlers came into the cave leading the boys' horses. The saddles were hanging over the backs of the animals.

'Look,' said Mfeni, 'there are two horses and three saddles. If Intambo finds out that Thulani was here, we will never get free. He will go out and bring his son back.'

Intambo came over to the two boys.

'Why are there three saddles and only two horses?' he asked.

'One of our friends is riding up to the cave tonight,' Mfeni replied. 'He wanted to ride bareback, so we brought his saddle for him.'

'I don't believe you,' shouted Intambo.

'It's true, Intambo,' said Mfeni. 'Dirkie's father told us to bring the third saddle. You know he doesn't like us to ride bareback for a long distance.'

Intambo nodded his head slowly, but he was not certain they were telling the truth. He looked at them for a long time.

'All right, I'll believe you, but one of the men will sit in the outside cave and watch for your friend.'

He spoke to one of the brightly blanketed men. He called another of the rustlers who ran down the cave towards the waterfall. Intambo came back to the boys with three of the rustlers.

'These men will watch you until we know what we will do with you,' Intambo said.

'If you hurt us,' Mfeni shouted, 'you will never escape.'

'Stop talking and do what you're told,' Intambo said angrily.

The rustlers pushed the boys against the wall of the cave, and then sat watching them. Dirkie could see the cattle grazing quietly outside the cave. He wondered how many of them belonged to his father.

◇

Thulani was very frightened and very cold. The trees were all around him. He decided to follow them down the hill until he came to a farm. He knew if he went down he would be going in the right direction.

He rode on keeping the trees close to him. He wiped his eyes, trying not to cry. He knew he had to be brave, but he was still only a young boy.

Chapter Eight

It was growing late on Sunday and the van der Riet family were becoming worried about the three boys. Dirkie and Mfeni always came home before sunset. Farmer van der Riet had phoned the police to ask for their help. He came into the kitchen where Jane and Helena were sitting, his bush-hat on his head.

'I'll start now, Jane,' he said. 'Zonke and his men will ride in the direction the boys went.'

The phone rang loudly in the next room. The farmer ran to answer it.

He listened for a minute and then asked some questions. Then he put the phone down.

'Well,' asked Jane, 'who was that?'

'That was that new man,' the farmer replied. 'He's bought the farm at Kloof Nek. Well, Thulani arrived at his farm this morning. He got lost trying to find the way from the camp last night.'

'Where are Dirkie and Mfeni?' Jane cried.

'I'm coming to that,' her husband replied. 'They were camping in a cave when Dirkie and Mfeni heard a strange noise. They went to find out what it was.'

'Well,' asked his wife, 'what happened?'

'Thulani doesn't know, Jane. The boys never

came back. Thulani was frightened and rode off.'

'Can he show you where the cave is?' Jane was very worried now.

'The farmer is bringing him back now,' her husband replied. 'But we'll start a search party at once. I have an idea where the cave is.'

Farmer van der Riet did not really know where the cave was. He just hoped that Thulani would remember.

Thandi and *Ukhulu* Sipho were both very worried. Zonke had ridden off with Farmer van der Riet. Sipho had wanted to go, but Zonke had said no. He sat under his *isiphuku* looking angry. Thandi had gone to talk to the other women. It was getting dark, there was no fire and food had been forgotten.

◇

Mfeni and Dirkie were now tied up against the wall. One man guarded them. The Basuto had started to move the cattle as soon as it became dark. They could not free the boys until all the cattle had gone.

They had been in the cave now for a day. Mfeni was surprised that they had not seen Intambo again.

'He has gone and left us,' said Mfeni to Dirkie. Dirkie's eyes filled with tears.

'When all the cattle have gone, they will leave us to die,' Dirkie said. 'Only Thulani knows about the cave. Why didn't he bring help?'

Mfeni was close to tears too, but he tried to be brave.

'Don't worry,' he said. 'Your Pa and my *Baba* will come soon, then I'll feel sorry for those rustlers.'

But Mfeni was afraid Thulani would not find the cave again. The Basuto would try to get the cattle into the mountains while it was still dark. They would leave the boys to die. Even if they untied themselves, they would never get back to the farm.

Mfeni tried to get comfortable. The ropes were hurting his hands and ankles. Dirkie's ankles were badly swollen. They were both very tired.

◇

The dog at *Ukhulu*'s feet suddenly started to growl. It got up and ran to the entrance to the kraal. Outside the mealies grew as tall as a man.

'Who's there?' shouted Sipho. There was no answer, but the dog was still barking.

'Who's there?' *Ukhulu* shouted again. 'Let me see you.'

'It's Intambo, *Ukhulu*,' said a voice.

'What do you want, you son of a dog?' the old man shouted. 'Get away before I use my spear on you.'

Intambo came into the kraal.

'Get out! Get out!' shouted Sipho angrily.

'Please don't shout,' Intambo begged. 'I don't want anyone to see me. I've come about your grandson Mfeni and his friend.'

'Aah, so you are behind this, you *inyoka*,' said Sipho. 'What has happened to my grandson and the *Inkosi*'s boy?'

'Listen, old man,' Intambo said, 'if you make any more noise, I'll go. Then you will never find them.'

'Speak quickly or I'll run my spear through you,' Sipho ordered.

Intambo explained why he had come.

◇

The farmer from Kloof Nek brought Thulani home after everyone had gone. Jane made them coffee and then asked Thulani dozens of questions about Dirkie and Mfeni. She could see that Thulani did not know the way back to the cave.

'Don't worry, Mrs van der Riet,' the farmer said, 'your husband knows this land like he knows the

'Please don't shout,' Intambo begged.

palm of his hand. He will soon find your son and his friend. I'll go back now and start a search from my farm. We'll follow the line of trees Thulani was talking about.'

Jane took the farmer to his Land Rover.

Chapter Nine

The moon came out from behind a cloud. Two riders were galloping up the valley towards the dark mountains. The first rider wore a shirt and trousers. The second rider looked like a warrior from a Royal Zulu *impi*.

He was wearing his battle dress. Round his forehead was a band of otter skin. Two plumes from the sakabula bird were stuck in the band on either side of his head. Down the back of his head hung a split bunch of ostrich feathers, and he had a feather from the blue crane in the centre of his forehead. Large bunches of white cow-tails hung from his neck down his back and chest. He wore a short kilt of Civet cat with green monkeys' skins tied at his waist and reaching down to his knees. He carried his white battle shield and his short stabbing spear. The warrior sat straight and strong in the saddle. The other rider shivered with fear when he looked at this warrior from the past.

Mfeni woke up when he heard the strange sounds coming from the passage to the cave. He saw two or three Basuto around the smoky fire, staring with looks of fear on their faces. For a moment Mfeni wondered what had woken him. Then he heard it again. It was the sound of loud chanting and the clip-clop of horses' hooves.

'Wake up, Dirkie,' he whispered. Dirkie sat up and stared all around him. The air in the cave was thick with smoke and the flames threw huge shadows on the walls. The sounds were closer now and the chanting sound was quite clear.

'What is it?' Dirkie asked, looking frightened.

'It's the battle-cry of the Zulu warrior,' replied Mfeni. 'My grandfather has sung it to me many times. It must be the *Izitonga*. The spirits look after the tribe in times of trouble.'

'That's silly, Mfeni,' said Dirkie, but a shiver of fear ran down his back.

The Basuto were standing at the opening to the cave. They were looking down the passage, terrified by the sound of the war-cry.

The boys could not move, so they lay watching the dark opening. Dirkie grew more afraid, but Mfeni was smiling. He was certain it was the *Izitonga*.

What they finally saw in the opening made the Basuto turn and run, their eyes staring with terror.

Sitting on his horse was a great Zulu warrior. His white shield was gleaming in the firelight. The feathers on his head fluttered as he moved. The sight of him would frighten any enemy.

When he saw the Basuto running away, the

Sitting on his horse was a great Zulu warrior.

warrior let out another war-cry and rode after them. When the cattle and goats and sheep saw him outside, they tried to escape. Some of them came into the cave and ran towards the opening. But another rider appeared and the animals turned again, almost trampling on the two boys. It was Thulani's father, Intambo.

'Intambo!' Dirkie shouted in surprise.

'Where has that silly old man gone?' Intambo said angrily.

'The *Izitonga* you mean?' Mfeni asked.

'That's not the *Izitonga*,' Intambo replied, 'that's your grandfather. He's come to fight the whole Basuto nation.'

Mfeni and Dirkie looked at each other in surprise.

'*Ukhulu?*' they said together. Could that great warrior in his battledress, sitting so proudly on his horse be their *Ukhulu*? *Ukhulu* was a toothless old man who sat beneath the orange tree.

The warrior came back into the cave and stopped in front of the two boys. He gave them a Zulu salute, his spear held high in the air.

'*Bayete!*' he cried. 'You are free to go, young prisoners.'

'Stop playing games, old man,' said Intambo. 'Remember what you promised.'

Sipho pointed his spear at Intambo's throat.

'Speak politely to a warrior of the Undi people, you son of a rat,' he said. 'One more word and I will open your throat for you. Now untie these children.'

Intambo began to cut the ropes. Then he spoke to the old man again.

'You promised to help me,' he said.

Sipho got down from his horse. Although he was very tired, he still looked like a great warrior.

'You will listen to me,' he said to Intambo. 'Your brave friends have run away. You will go after them. Leave the Basuto horses and all the cattle and goats. Now go!'

'How will I get over the mountains without a horse?' Intambo asked.

'That is your business, you dog,' the old man said. 'Now go at once!'

He pointed his spear at Intambo again, and Intambo turned and ran.

Sipho turned to the boys and told them what had happened. They wanted to ask him questions. He told them he had to rest before they went back down the mountain. Soon all three were asleep. Sipho looked old and tired. His headdress and his white shield lay on the ground beside him. But still held tightly in his hand was his short spear.

Questions

1 What did Grandfather Sipho enjoy doing when he was sitting under the orange tree?
2 Explain the reason for the fight between Mfeni and Thulani. What did Sipho say was wrong with Thulani?
3 Why did Mfeni and Dirkie decide to explore the back of the cave?
4 What did Thulani do when the boys did not return? What happened to him?
5 What happened to Dirkie and Mfeni?
6 How were they finally rescued?

Activities

1 Draw a map of Africa. Put in the outline of your own country and colour it neatly. Now put in the country where this story comes from and colour it too. You can colour in the countries of the various stories you read in the JAWS series.
2 Have a class debate. The topic for the debate is – 'Fighting is bad'. Remember two people should speak for the motion (the topic) and two people should speak against it. Then the rest of the class can give their opinion. The class should then vote whether or not they agree with the motion.

Glossary

apologise (page 17) say that you are sorry
Basuto (page 24) people from Lesotho
bayete (page 57) I salute you
'Berg (page 33) Drakensberg Mountains in Natal in South Africa
calabash (page 23) the hard case of a vegetable used as a container
civilised (page 6) behaving peacefully and thinking in a modern way
impi (page 54) a band of Zulu warriors
Induna (page 1) foreman
Inkosi (page 6) chief
intendele (page 33) a quail
intombi (page 7) young girl
inyoka (page 51) snake
isagila (page 33) throwing stick with a knob on one end
isiphuku (page 18) large blanket or a cloak
Izitonga (page 41) ancestral spirits
phuthu (page 15) a kind of porridge
rustlers (page 20) people who steal cattle
sawubona (page 8) greetings
silhouetted (page 6) dark shadow against a light background
strutted (page 9) walked proudly

twilight (page 6) the time when it is just becoming dark

trampling (page 57) step on very heavily

Ukhulu (page 4) grandfather

umfana (page 3) young boy

umkhukha (page 30) sleeping mat

vain (page 14) admiring oneself

The Junior African Writers Series is designed to provide interesting and varied African stories both for pleasure and for study. There are five graded levels in the series.

Level 3 is for readers who have being studying English for five to six years. The content and language have been carefully controlled to increase fluency in reading.

Content The plots are linear in development and only the characters and information central to the storyline are introduced. Chapters divide the stories into focused episodes and the illustrations help the reader to picture the scenes.

Language Reading is a learning experience and although the choice of words is carefully controlled, new words, important to the story, are also introduced. These are contextualised, recycled through the story and explained in the glossary. The sentences contain a maximum of three short clauses.

Glossary Difficult words which learners may not know and which are not made clear in the text or illustrations have been listed alphabetically at the back of the book. The definitions refer to the way the word is used in the story and the page reference is for the word's first use.

Questions and **Activities** The questions give useful comprehension practice and ensure that the reader has followed and understood the story. The activities develop themes and ideas introduced and can be done as pairwork or groupwork in class, or as homework.

Resource Material Further resources are being developed to assist in the teaching of reading with JAWS titles.

Other JAWS titles at Level 3

The Young Builder, Gillian Leggat, 0 435 89237 1

Tikrit, Chris Burchell, 0 435 89238 X

The Artist and the Bully, Gillian Leggat, 0 435 89233 9

The Young Detectives, Yaw Ababio Boateng, 0 435 89234 7

Lindiwi Finds a Way, Eileen Molver, 0 435 89235 5